What do People get when they get you?

TOSHA EVANS

All rights reserved. No part of this publication may be reproduced, distributed, or transmitted in any form or by any means, including photocopying, recording, or other electronic or mechanical methods, without the prior written permission of the publisher, except in the case of brief quotations embodied in critical reviews and certain other noncommercial uses permitted by copyright law. For permission requests, email the publisher, include "Attention: Permission Coordinator," in the subject line at tosharevans@yahoo.com.

Copyright 2020 by: TE - LIVE WELL MINISTRIES
ISBN: 978-0-9973705-2-2
Printed in the United States of America

Cover Designs: Derin
Front Cover Photo: KendyKam Photography
About the Author Photo: The Moments

Disclaimer: Names and identifying details have been changed to protect the privacy of individuals.

DEDICATION

I am forever grateful to my parents. It is hard to wrap my mind around the depth of sacrifice that they endured for me, my sisters, and my brother. I can recall at least a million life lessons that we acquired as a result of watching them live and serve as examples over the years. To name a few, their commitment to ensure that we had a solid ministry foundation, that we were hard workers and the importance of helping others. Thanks, be unto God for their seeds sown into our lives. We are successful because of them. With love and sincerest gratitude, I dedicate this book to you both.

ACKNOWLEDGMENTS

Thank you to a host of family members and friends. I am honored that God chose me to be connected to each of you. It is true... *"iron sharpens iron"* - your strength and encouragement have helped me persevere and pen this book. I will be forever grateful for the love and support that you extended during the writing process. Thank you for pre-reading, sharing feedback and your prayers. Thank you again and again.

PROLOGUE

Your greatest struggle is not with people nor your circumstances. The greatest struggle that you will ever encounter is in your mind. This war is silent and subtle. Although we are yet to meet, I am sure the struggles that you have encountered have left you with invisible wounds. Invisible to the eye, but those wounds have likely left deep mental and emotional scarring. This book will support you in taking a deep dive within to expose those wounds and tread the path toward healing.

What Do People Get – When They Get You contains seven independent principles that will support you in your journey toward self-discovery and transformation. The principles will inspire you to take an introspective look at who you really are and will motivate you to scale the cliffs of your mind in hopes of enhancing or experiencing a better quality of life.

The wisdom within has most certainly been pivotal in my life's transformation. Dig in!

INTRODUCTION

I have to ask...What Do People Get - When They Get You?

A riveting question...I know. Chances are, this thought has never crossed your mind. This is because most people occupy a space of believing, seeking, and wanting. When we are in the mindset of receiving, our expectations are heightened, and we are often heavily focused on other people and have low (or no) focus on ourselves. We want what we want, and we want it NOW. Not to mention, we have extremely high expectations for the people and things around us to measure up and to be on point. And this is great, but, what do you offer out? Have you ever stopped to think about what you are bringing to the table? Have you ever stopped to think about how you are received? Have you ever stopped to think about the impact that you make when you walk into a room or when you leave a room?

This book will inspire you to take a deep dive within. Afterall, everything starts and stops with you. The Real You! Again, I ask, "What Do People Get - When They Get _____? (add your name in the blank space)

I put together a small focus group when writing this book because I wanted to gather the reactions of people regarding the riveting question. 98% of the group looked stunned, followed by stares of panic…which I found to be hilarious. Then I received a few one liner's, "Ummmm", "WOW", "This is a bombshell", "This is a lot to take in", "I pondered on this for days…and I still don't have an answer". All of which were exactly what I was looking for: honesty and rawness. What I find to be even more interesting, is that when I asked those same people to share their expectations in regard to careers, relationships etc.; their list rolled right off their tongues with very little thought. They had a clear line of sight of external factors, but they had a blurred line of sight as to who they were or what they had to offer.

I volley the question to you again, What do People Get - When They Get You? What's behind your polished or unpolished exterior? Does the question have you wide eyed and puzzled, clutching your pearls, or at ease because you are able to respond with confidence? Do people get the same you in every situation? How consistent are you in every area of your life? Do your core values transfer into the various roles of you as a parent, sibling, employee, business owner, brief encounters, in the community, during a season of singleness or marriage? Regardless of your response to the questions, I am so grateful that this book has found you. In Jesus' name I believe it will encourage you to view your life from a different perspective. Afterall, each day you wake up - you are gifted with another opportunity to impact your life and those around you. Whether it's a brief encounter or long standing personal/professional relationship know that you are making an impact. With this in mind, be sure and make a positive, lasting, and impressionable one. Here's the answer to the riveting question: The core values that People Should Get - When They Get You...are kindness, patience, forgiveness, love, support and thoughtfulness. Integrity. Joy. Good character. Inspiration. Hope. A Positive Influence. Compassion. Empathy. In contrast, you should not project your criticism, judgments, bitterness, envy, insulting or demeaning spirit on to others. The negative residue (such as your pain, limitations, insecurities, guilt, failures, negative perception of life or your fears) from previous experiences, often manifests in the form of bullying, passive aggressiveness, rudeness, verbal, emotional or physical abuse. Always remember, the people around you are recipients to how you manage life's highs or lows. And, it isn't fair or ideal for you to project that type of energy onto others. Chances are, if you are sharing that type of energy, you have received it. Know that you have the power to break the cycle. If you aren't already, become conscientious of this and commit to adding value which helps to build individuals up. Here's the deal, at the end of the day - you have high expectations and standards of others…decide to be the standard. Remember – you will always reap what you sow.

This book will help you to gain a better perspective and will add value to your life. The more value you add to your life, the more you can add to other people's lives. Enjoy.

You Can't Fix - What You Can't Face.
~ Tosha Evans

What do People get when they get you?

TOSHA EVANS

CONTENTS

DEDICATION.. i
ACKNOWLEDGEMENTS... ii
PROLOUGE.. iii
INTRODUCTION.. iv

PRINCIPLE ONE: IT STARTS IN THE MIND...................... 1

PRINCIPLE TWO:
TELL YOURSELF THE TRUTH FIRST................................15

PRINCIPLE THREE: TAKE OUT THE T.R.A.S.H (Trauma | Resentment| Anxiety | Stress |Hinderances..........................23

PRINCIPLE FOUR:
WHAT YOU DON'T OVERCOME – YOU BECOME...........39

PRINCIPLE FIVE:
YOU vs. The Other YOU... 51

PRINCIPLE SIX:
I AM CREATED FOR THIS...63

PRINCIPLE SEVEN:
LIVE WELL..67

PRINCIPLE ONE
IT STARTS IN THE MIND

Your beliefs become your thoughts, your thoughts become your words, your words become your actions, your actions become your habits, your habits become your values, your values become your destiny. ~ Mahatma Gandhi

What Do People Get When They Get Your – Beliefs, Thoughts, Words, Actions, Habits or Values? It is important that you are able to answer this question, because these elements are the essence of you. **Think About It:** Do you evoke a positive or negative connotation of these traits? Your ability or inability to answer reveals your level of self-awareness. It is often easier to pinpoint whether these traits are on point when we are considering an associate or a loved one. However, it is imperative that you are aware of how you measure up as well. Your level of self-awareness is linked to your self-worth and both are connected to what you believe to be true about yourself. As within, so without. Meaning, you will always project out what lies within you.

What you believe, the thoughts that you think, every word that you speak, your actions, values and habits start in your MIND. Your mind is similar to that of a melting pot that houses all your past experiences and future endeavors. And this melting pot, flashes images and sends you notifications every second of every day. Have you ever stopped to think about – what you are thinking about? Do your thoughts bring you peace or do they hold you hostage? Your mind is powerful. Your mindset is the driving force for every action and reaction. It affects the way that you lead your life. Within this principle let's examine two key areas: A mindset of Faith and Your Perspective.

Your Mindset is Everything!

Choose a mindset of Faith. A mindset of faith does not mean that you won't be faced with challenges or hardships. Trust me life will continue to happen but, by faith you have the power to overcome every trial that is behind and ahead of you. A mindset of faith strengthens your beliefs and offers thoughts of peace. There is nothing like peace in your mind. Although we are yet to meet, what I know for sure is that you have endured hardships and challenges. And, those challenges vary from self-esteem issues, feelings of being overlooked, undervalued, ostracized, abuse, unforgiveness and more. Be careful to not allow your past experiences to define you but allow God's word to define who you are. This will tread the path toward healing your heart and mind. It most certainly has been pivotal in my life's transformation. A mindset of faith will positively impact the thoughts that you think.

    In my quest to learn more about mental health and the mind, I stumbled upon a Health and Wellness article a few years ago and what I discovered blew me away. Experts report: Individuals think approximately 12,000 - 60,000 thoughts per day. Did you get that? 12,000 – 60,000 thoughts each day. Of those thousands of thoughts, 80% are negative, and 95% are repeated within your mind day in and day out. Take a moment here to think about the DOMINATE thoughts that run rampant in your mind. Do your DOMINATE thoughts inspire you to create, build, or dream? Or do your thoughts have you imprisoned by fear, worried and/or weighed down by what other people think of you? Learning to manage your mind and the thoughts that you think can result in you Living Your Life Well.

Perspective!
The proper perspective will help you to navigate thru life's highs such as new beginnings, promotions and moments of bliss. Afterall, when life is great, we feel great and we want more of it. But, be ready for the lows that life will bring like the challenges within your relationships, financial hardships, the loss of a loved one and more. The ability to remain hopeful is key. Hope helps you to rise above the hardship and this mindset enables you to overcome anything that life presents. This is your source of power! With every challenge that you endure negative thoughts and

feelings of hopelessness will surface but, your ability to detach from negative thoughts and channel that energy toward the proper perspective will change your life. You generally have no control over the circumstances that arise, the hard times are unavoidable and you do not have the option to escape the struggle but you can control your mindset and the way that you respond. Earlier, we referenced your mind to that of a melting pot that houses all of your past experiences and future endeavors. **This is a direct link to why the 12,000 – 60,000 thoughts that you think daily is vital.** Those thoughts impact your perspective. Choose to respond with the right perspective and remember that everything that happens in your life is on purpose and for a purpose. Each and every challenge is a learning opportunity. Choose to respond to challenges with the Word of God instead of responding with your feelings. Imagine if your 12,000 – 60,000 thoughts were laced with God's word. Imagine the impact that this would have on your perspective and the healing of your mind.

Having Perspective and Faith will change the game for you. Here is how…there is a short list of things that are guaranteed in life. Trials and Hardships are on that short list. Since you know this…Remain ready. Remain aware. Remain mindful. Like most things in life when you are prepared – you position yourself to respond differently. For example, when meteorologists inform us that inclement weather is coming to our area; the smart action to take is to respond accordingly. From stocking our homes with food, supplies, seeking safety - by means of sheltering in place and even cases of possible evacuation. This mindset of preparedness will prove to be effective and beneficial. Similar to not having control of inclement weather, you often will not have control of what is to come but, it is vital that you are ready and mindful of your response. Your takeaway from the things that happen will do one of two things nourish or hurt you mentally and emotionally. And this takeaway impacts your Beliefs, Thoughts, Words Habits and Actions. All of which are the essence of you. Remember everything starts in the mind.

A flashback at my Lack of Faith and Perspective...

I was twelve years old when I tried out for the basketball team. My crew back then consisted of me and two other girls. I remember having so much fun with Nessa and Tia. We did everything together. Not to mention, we participated in our Junior High School talent show and WON!!! Three ambitious young girls – ready to take on the world by way of the 7th grade...lol. So, we decided to try out for the basketball team. They were athletes by nature. I mean, they were skilled at every sport. Let's just say...I wasn't. Although not a skilled athlete, I have always been a hard worker.

So, we decided to try out for the basketball team. Oh boy! The challenge was on. Let me be clear the physical aspects of tryouts were a breeze.

Drills, rebounding, running through offensive and defensive plays...I was able to hang with no issues. The issue I had - was BELIEVING that I would actually make the team. I wasn't familiar with the term self-esteem back then. I just knew I would find myself shrinking when it came time to show up in various aspects of my life. Subconsciously, I was comparing myself to the other girls that were naturally talented. Comparing yourself to others is a dangerous game. I, was totally ignoring the fact that I was on point with conditioning, doing the drills, running the sprints and running a 7.48 mile (very proud of that especially considering I wasn't an athlete, but, haven't ran at that pace since Junior High...lol); the only thing that I was focused on was whether or not my name would be listed on the coaches door. Back then, "The Who made TEAM A and TEAM B" was posted outside the door of the coach's office. I was terrified of my name not being listed. So, when I say "It starts in the mind" it's true. Here is an example of how it starts in the mind and an example of one of my early rendezvous' s with self-sabotage. Because of low self-esteem and a fearful mindset, I proceeded to talk to the coach after the final practice. I waited for everyone to leave the locker room. Nervous as all get-out, I knocked on the door of Coach's office. She greeted me and asked, "What's up". I spent more time looking at the floor as I was speaking, than looking at her but, I managed to mumble out "I don't want to play on the team." She was absolutely stunned! I am sure she was thinking why in the world would someone show up to practice and workout like a maniac only to decide not to play. She stumbled, on her words and said - What? As if she didn't hear me the first time. I repeated myself. Then she responded with asking "Why, Tosha"; you have been doing such a good job? Then, I had a thought of "What in the world" she thinks I'm doing a good job? But that moment was brief and overshadowed by feelings of shame since I had already kicked myself off the team. I will never forget the huge boulder of regret that settled into my stomach in that moment. I maintained my stance and responded with "Oh no, I just want to be the team manager". I might add, that, I never - ever wanted to be the team manager, I just made that up in that moment. She looked at me with confusion and disappointment and said "Well, that's too bad – because you actually made the team". I was shocked again. **I'D ACTUALLY MADE THE TEAM!!** I wanted to cry. I was beyond crushed. I also wanted to be honest with her, but I was gripped with embarrassment and fear. So, I played it off as if it did not matter, thanked her and walked away.

    The season kicked off with me as the Team Manager and I was secretly miserable and devastated. To mask my truth, I did what I did best during those days, and that was minimize my feelings and acted like I was just fine. My friends were just as shocked and confused as Coach. My decision didn't make sense to them nor me. As I reflect, this experience taught me that my hard work ethic was indeed a strength. Hard work, drive and determination will create opportunities for you just like natural talent but, most importantly – I needed to believe in myself. Neither the Coach, Nessa nor Tia would ever know the truth. I would have to live with this poor decision that I'd made for the rest of my life. And, I have lived with this and many other unfortunate moments which were created due to my poor self-image and fearful mindset. Your mindset will always win. What they say is actually true…if you think you can't - you are right! And my 12,000 thoughts had me kick myself off the team. Again, I must repeat - I had actually made the team. Grateful that this memory no longer stings and that now I view this as a learning opportunity.

It is highly likely that you do not have my basketball experience. But you do have a story. It is likely that your story is laced with some type of insecurity. I am curious…have your thoughts ever held you hostage? Have you ever had a rendezvous with self-sabotage? Meaning…have you ever found yourself shrinking when it was time to show up in various aspects of your life? Have you ever suppressed your truth, or minimized your feelings? Have you ever been afraid to use your voice and speak up for what you want? Have you ever been gripped by embarrassment or secretly miserable? Have you ever acted as if something didn't matter – when it really did? Have you ever found yourself - comparing yourself to others? Although, we do not have the same story, it is likely that we share or shared these types of insecurities. Insecurities such as these used to get the best of me. They served as barriers that I willingly surrendered too - that was then. As a result of continuous hard work, prayer, fasting, a radical shift in mindset - my life and experiences are different, and my quality of life has positively transformed. It is an honor to pay it forward with this book. I purposely featured "It Starts In the Mind" as the first principle. It is unfortunate but insecurities are the driving force that keep many people held back in life. As mentioned earlier, the mind is a melting pot of ideas, insecurities, habits, previous experiences, and more. If you have not already, get a handle on this. Add this content to your personal development toolbox and watch your life transform.

Your Key Takeaways:

1. What Do People Get - When They Get a person who is thinking about what they are thinking?
2. Do you have thoughts that run rampant? Consider journaling for a minimum of ten minutes daily (the more time you put in, the better the results) starting today. This simple exercise will help you to gain control over your mind and the thoughts that may be running rampant.

PRINCIPLE TWO
TELL YOURSELF THE TRUTH FIRST!

Sometimes people do not want to hear the truth, because they do not want their illusions destroyed.
~ Friedrich Nietzsche

Be honest with yourself. Seems like an easy task, right? But how often do you take the time to get quiet and to listen to your inner self? How many times have you ignored your gut? What are your deficiencies? Why are you fearful? Why do you hold grudges? Why do you second guess yourself? What is keeping you from pursuing your dreams? How well do you really know yourself? Your greatest challenge isn't changing external things. Your greatest challenge will be for you to go within. And the first steps as you journey inward, is to be honest with yourself and getting to know who you are.

"Tell <u>YOURSELF</u> the Truth FIRST!" I was watching a documentary and an audio clip of the great Maya Angelo uttered these words and within an instant – my life changed. How? It challenged me to think about how often I had lied to myself about what was or wasn't important and how many times I'd denied my truth to accommodate something or someone else. Take a moment to think about your life, how satisfied are you with your personal or professional relationships? How many times have you lied to yourself? If you are currently doing so, imagine how great it would be to live and own your truth. That simple phrase serves as a key that can unlock the prison door that has been constructed by your thoughts. This trigger, "Tell Yourself the Truth First" challenged and gave me the courage to begin to explore the depths of…the REAL ME and it connected me with the ultimate – FREEDOM! Imagine the freedom to say, "yes" to healing from within, love, forgiveness and escaping the ruins of depression. Also, imagine the freedom to say, "no" to the mask of living a two-faced life, being manipulated by every genre of fear and concerned about what other people think. This freedom will birth a new strength within you that can transform your life.

Imagine really knowing who you are. Being sure of who you are is imperative because it helps you to value and appreciate yourself. Self-awareness is key. It is like being surrounded by a sphere and with that sphere you have the power to allow or not allow other people's emotions, thoughts, opinions and judgements to penetrate on to you. That layer of protection is a shield that serves with a dual purpose to build your esteem and strengthen your mindset. To put it plainly, knowing who you are gives you the courage to own the perspective that says– what matters most, is the opinion that I have of myself. THIS IS YOUR SOURCE OF POWER! Your ability to manage your emotions and your perspective will set you free and give you wings to rise above your challenges and the opinions of others.

Are you living your truth? If not, consider it. Because what they say is true…" The truth will set you Free". After all, you are the only one that is holding you back.

I've included a simple, yet effective exercise that will help you with your self-examination. It's a SWOT (Strengths, Weaknesses, Opportunities and Threats) Analysis for your life. SWOT is often referred to in business. In my opinion, it can and should also be applied to everyday life as well. After all, your life should be your business. Evaluating your strengths, weaknesses, opportunities and threats will be difficult and beneficial.

Grab a sheet of paper or make notes on your SWOT Analysis page (next page) . After you complete the exercise, fasten your seat belt and prepare to experience your life thru new lenses'. It's always enlightening and humbling when we identify areas of development. Take a moment to grab your favorite pen and answer at least one item in each category. The goal is to complete it, however, simply starting carries a lot of weight.

A SWOT Analysis of YOU
Strengths Weakness Opportunities Threats

Strengths: (positive characteristics)

1.

2.

3.

Weaknesses: (areas of improvement)

1.

2.

3.

Opportunities: (things you have access to but, may not be taking advantage of)

1.

2.

3.

Threats: (things that are preventing you from achieving your goals)

1.

2.

3.

Congratulations…on kicking off your SWOT Analysis! Self-discovery is key to transformation. One thing that we all have in common is the need to grow in various aspects of our lives. No matter how old you are or what you have accomplished, the common bond that we share in is that we are ever evolving; and with that creates opportunities for continued learning and development. Be mindful that as you change your strengths, weaknesses, opportunities and threats will change as well. Be sure to revisit the SWOT as the seasons of your life change.

Key Takeaways:

1. For the next 30 days, commit to setting aside time at the beginning or end of your day to get quiet and listen to yourself. Start by setting a timer for 10 minutes, silence all of your devices and retreat to a private space where you won't be disturbed or distracted. Have your journal handy to capture all that is revealed.
2. What did the S.W.O.T teach you about yourself?

PRINCIPLE THREE
TAKE OUT THE T.R.A.S.H

Knowing others is intelligence; knowing yourself is true wisdom. Mastering others is strength; mastering yourself is true power
~ J. Paulsen

Ready to experience PEACE and FREEDOM? Then, take out the T.R.A.S.H. This will change your life! Trauma, Resentment, Anxiety, Stress and Hinderances are derived from the previous challenges and hardships that you have experienced. Imagine completely clearing your heart, mind and spirit from this debris and clutter. It is possible! And, it is time! If you allow the debris of T.R.A.SH to be housed in your heart, mind and spirit - they will weigh you down. We depart every experience with some sort of impact. The good experiences yield positive impacts and the negative experiences yield some form of T.R.A.S.H or other negative impacts. And, when we encounter negative experiences, we go through them and when it's over – we are glad they are over! Being out of those situations offers relief but, we must be mindful of the healing process. The healing process is imperative to your growth and development. If you don't take time to heal from trauma, resentment, anxiety, stress and/or hinderances it gets compacted within you. This weight negatively impacts your thoughts, feelings, emotions and the essence of you. You go to sleep with it, you wake up with it and you carry this weight throughout each day. You cannot continue to carry this type of weight as it holds you back. It impacts your relationships with others and the relationship that you have with yourself. This type of weight creates and secures a wedge of distance between you and your dreams.

One of the keys to mastering YOU is by T.R.A.S.H removal. Let's dive into The Why and The How.

The Why:

When you don't remove the T.R.A.S.H. it impacts every aspect of you. Especially the THOUGHTS that you think. Let's look at the science behind it. Each and Every thought that you think releases a chemical into your body. This chemical release can be a negative stress hormone (Increased levels of Cortisol) or a positive release (Serotonin/Dopamine). **Think About It:** every thought that you think is positively or negatively impacting you. Take a moment to take this in, awareness of this can change the trajectory of your life. Your thoughts impact your self-esteem, your health and your overall well-being. Don't take your thoughts for granted. And, don't allow your thoughts to manipulate and control you. You have the power to take control of your life and mental health by getting control of the thoughts that you think. Principle One: shared the reference that 12,000 - 60,000 thoughts that the average person thinks each day. Again, each thought that you think releases a positive or negative chemical into your mind that goes through your body. Imagine 12,000 – 60,000 chemical releases into your mind on Monday, Tuesday, Wednesday, Thursday, Friday, Saturday and Sunday. This is heavy. This explains a lot about where you are mentally, emotionally, physically, spiritually and financially.

Additionally, choosing to take out the T.R.A.S.H (which impacts your thoughts) can positively or negatively impact your social behavior, mood, learning, appetite and/or well-being. As well as your immune system, digestive system and more. Your commitment to doing the work of improving your mental health impacts your physical health as well.

The How:
The courage to take out the T.R.A.S.H will relieve you of worry, stress and resentment which are by-products of T.R.A.S.H. This relief will afford you the opportunity to experience better mental and physical health. The upside to taking out the T.R.A.S.H yields great rewards but, it requires work. This principle is not to make you think that - if you think positive – positive things will happen. It will require everything within you to change your life. The commitment to experiencing a lasting change in your mind and life will require you to surrender your old

thoughts and habits. After – all, You Can't Fix – What You Can't Face and not to mention your T.R.A.S.H is doing you a disservice.

Surrendering is pivotal to your transformation. When you surrender you relinquish the control and burden of trying to fix things. It's a place where you humble yourself before God and allow Him to lead, heal and transform you. The act of surrendering can be a physical posture of kneeling or a mental release. Both postures are a call out that can express something like: "God I cannot do this without you". You literally, cast every care (unforgiveness, fear, negative thoughts etc.) and you leave every worry behind. When you release all the T.R.A.S.H this clears all the debris and clutter. Allowing wholeness, new thoughts, and new habits to birth within you. This exchange from old to new is truly a life changing experience. You begin to see yourself the way He sees you, which strengthens your self-esteem. This metamorphosis is powerful and euphoric, but it must be maintained. Ever wonder why, someone with thinking patterns: like addictions to shopping, tobacco, food, pornography, social media, alcohol, drugs, unhealthy relationships or gambling revert back to old habits? Their desire or thought for the "thing" will remain strong, until that person replaces that desire with new thoughts. This is where the grit comes in. It's denying yourself of the habit. Not to mention the habit serves as an escape, which leaves individuals unsatisfied and longing. Addictions are a byproduct of not taking out your T.R.A.S.H, they offer a temporary escape from various forms of trauma, resentment, anxiety, stress and hinderances. The escapes never satisfy they only pacify. However, a complete change of mind that is undergirded with the word of God offers an opportunity for lasting change. Creating a new normal such as being plugged into His word and committing to renewing your mind will birth new desires and thoughts within you. It is truly the divine exchange of swapping your old thinking patterns and desires for His peace. A bonus for the new life is the benefit of The Living Water which heals and satisfies. Living Water represents the grace and spirit of God which is signified by water. Because of its cleansing and purifying nature through faith and hope, **the Living Water has the power to cleanse you from all addictions, areas of brokenness, low self-esteem and various forms of sin.** This is the process of treading the path of lasting change. This is most certainly a process. Making the decision to change your life is not a onetime act. You literally don't clock out, it's a process of being mindful of your thoughts every second of every day. The healing process is powerful and two-fold. When you heal it transforms you and serves as Hope to others.

Deciding not to deal with your T.R.A.S.H may seem like an easier route to take, especially considering the healing process is a life-long commitment. With this mindset, people often decide to mask the T.R.A.S.H with a "new fix" like; relationships, they buy new toys (cars, homes, gadgets) or start new businesses or careers etc. in hopes that this will be the fix for their life. But the T.R.A.S.H remains. And the T.R.A.S.H intertwines and muddies up the "new fix". Remember, As within – So without. What's within you will always surface. In order to move forward effectively, you must face your issues. This is the truest setup for success. The courage and doing the work of taking out the T.R.A.S.H helps you to heal and become whole.

In the earlier chapters of my life I carried my T.R.A.S.H into new seasons, new relationships and new jobs. And, in those days – I found myself wondering why I continued to yield the same results. What I didn't realize was that the days, seasons and situations were changing but, I wasn't.

Here's a look back: At my first rodeo with being BRAVE enough to tread the path toward healing and T.R.A.S.H removal...

I remember being rushed to the emergency room because I'd passed out at work. There, I was lying on the floor of the office. I had no pulse. I spent several days in the hospital. The doctors ran test after test and found nothing. What they didn't know, was that my body was responding to the tremendous amount of stress that had been dominate throughout my life. I was completely oblivious to the impact that stress can cause to one's mind and body. I'd read articles and watched movies about people having mental breakdowns but, never in one million years would I have imagined that would be me. I was always seen as outgoing, ambitious, hardworking and fun to be around. People would never have associated the word stress with me. But like many people, I was skilled at suppressing pain, sporting the mask of perfection and portraying that I lived in a picturesque world. My collapse and breakdown were brought on by, absorbing years of mental, emotional and verbal abuse. I was used to being rejected, demeaned, neglected, overlooked and mistreated. Nothing to be proud of but - that was my norm. Through the years of being, beat down mentally and emotionally, I became numb to the blows that created my invisible wounds. Talk about a scary place to be, when you no longer feel pain, hurt or disappointment. It was as if I was lost within myself. In this dark space, I lacked courage, I was terrified to use my voice and to speak up for myself; it gets worse - I had no standards or expectations as to how I should be treated. As a result of being mentally and verbally beat down; what I thought about myself ranked low as well.

As a result of the mental torment, I found myself living an unfulfilled life and trying to be someone else. Which is interesting because someone would generally long to be someone else if they didn't like who they were in the first place. During those chapters of my life, I was the opposite; I had no idea of who I was so, living the life of a chameleon was common to me. Again, nothing to be proud of but, that was my truth. I smiled when I was actually sad. I was used to saying that I was ok, when I really wasn't. I was skilled at dismissing and suppressing pain. We generally handle difficult experiences in one of two ways; we explode or implode. I was the imploder. Again, nothing to brag about. I Internalized pain, which birthed depression within me, and both seriously impacted my mental, physical, health and well-being. There were so many things that I didn't know in the earlier years of my life. And, it's true what they say, "what you don't know, can hurt you".

Decades passed before, I sought help. One morning, bright and early, I phoned my sister and told her I was ready to see a therapist. I was ready to move forward with my life, but I knew in order to put the past behind me…sweeping it under the rug was no longer an option. I had to face it! I was determined to get to the root of why I had been so timid and why I'd allowed myself to be bullied and demeaned. This was a major turning point in my life. I had no idea of what to expect from my sessions with a therapist, but what I knew for sure - was that something needed to change and that was ME! To say that I was uncomfortable during the first few sessions, was an understatement. Imagine two people sitting on opposite sides of a room, although her eyes and spirit were calming, I still felt uneasy. I was uneasy because facing my past meant I'd have to TALK about it. This was difficult for me because my voice had been muzzled by fear for many years. The very idea of sitting down and reflecting on my life was one thing but, talking about it was another animal. Being silent and choosing to suppress my feelings in the earlier days were coping mechanisms that I heavily relied on. And, showing up for these sessions meant that I had to separate from that mindset.

Dr. Lez (my therapist) proceeded to set the timer and utters "So tell me about you"? I responded with silence. Her next question, "Tosha, tell me a little bit about why you are here?" We had a bit of a stare off going for what seemed liked several minutes. I appreciated her patience as I tried to find the words that could articulate an answer to either question. At first nothing came to mind. Secretly, I was hoping that my silence would motivate her to continue with the session without asking me questions or I was also ok with walking out the door and not finishing the session. She clearly missed my silent S.O.S. She gave me a comforting look that suggested, "You can do this". The only words that I could conjure up were "that I'd been through a lot and that I didn't know where to begin." Tears began to stream from my eyes, it was in that moment that I was no longer numb to the torment that created my invisible wounds. In that moment, I'd reunited with the pain that I'd skillfully ignored and suppressed for many years. And, boy did it hurt! The intention to take responsibility for my life and get help was a double-edged sword. Because it meant I was treading a path toward healing but, having to revisit the dark places that created the wounds in the first place was a lot to take in. It gets deeper, the muzzle had been removed. Actually, hearing my voice utter my truth was also a lot to take in as well. This is because, I'd previously occupied a space of denial and the courage to talk about my T.R.A.S.H was the beginning of me finding my voice. It was one thing to barely survive those dark days, and it is another thing to have to relive them. Dr. Lez taught me that this was the path toward healing.

It is truly God's grace that has saved my life and I am grateful to have taken a detour from self-sabotage, neglect and abuse toward a life of wellness, wholeness, purpose and truth. Not having a pulse, suffering in silence, identity crisis, depression and battling with poor mental health are just a few areas that God's grace has healed within me. Seeing a therapist was one of the hardest things that I have ever done but, also one of the most rewarding. I realize that every day that I wake up is a gift - honoring God with my life and renewing my mind daily helps me to continue to evolve. The grit and courage to take out my T.R.A.S.H has transitioned my life toward purpose and truth. If I can do it – You can do it!

Like me, every day that you wake up is a gift as well. And, your journey continues with the decisions that you make each day. Here are a few resources that will support you with T.R.A.S.H removal: journaling, exercising, seeing a therapist, reading your bible or devotionals. You can also plug into encouraging media outlets that positively feed your mind and spirit. Choose one of those options or all. Remember in order to experience a change, YOU have to change!

Key takeaways:

1. **Think About it:** Since you don't want other people's T.R.A.S.H, be proactive and ensure that you are not giving your T.R.A.S.H to others as well.
2. **Think About It:** Each person thinks approximately 12,000 – 60,000 per day. Each thought releases a (positive or negative) chemical. This impacts your mind and body which impacts the quality of your life. Monitor your thoughts daily, the quality of your life depends on it.

PRINCIPLE FOUR

WHAT YOU DON'T OVERCOME - YOU BECOME

Between stimulus and response there is space. In that space is our power to choose our response. In our response lies our growth and our freedom ~ Viktor Frankl

The relationship that you have with God is the most important relationship that you will ever have. As it defines who YOU are. It is the direct link to your self-worth, your relationships with everyone and everything in your life. The image below expresses this hierarchy. The arrows represent the correlation of God as the lead and then you and everything else. The "everything else" represents your other relationships that's (you as a spouse, parent, sibling, business owner, employee, friendships etc.)

Looking at your life today, where does God rank? Where do you rank? Where does everything else rank? Take a moment to populate the image below with your responses.

Order is fundamental to every aspect of your life. There is order to your morning routine, to the way that you prepare meals, to preparing to go on vacations and more. Order is also imperative to your daily walk and your personal growth. Ensuring that God is the lead offers a life of peace and balance which filters into every aspect of your life. Ever wonder why you have become overwhelmed with the demands and pressures of life? Have you ever felt lost or alone? Chances are the answer is yes and yes. When you are in relationship with Him the demands and pressures of life are easier to bear because your perspective shifts from you being in control to Him handling the heavy lifting. And, when you are in relationship with Him you take comfort in knowing that you are not alone, nor have you ever been alone. Although He isn't present in the physical sense of a person, His presence and His grace manifests in many forms. The mere fact that your eyes opened this morning is an example of His grace and the fact that you have overcome the challenges that you have faced is another example. The commitment to cultivate a relationship with God provides an anchoring that is second to none. This anchoring helps to solidify who you are, and it supports your perspective toward challenges. This perspective will help you to Overcome the offenses/offender that you have faced vs Becoming the offense/offender that wronged you.

Take a moment to reflect back on your paths of hardships. That could be the hardships of marriage, divorce, poor self-image, abuse, and/or financial issues etc. Now imagine that you are traveling through those previous hardships via a path and that path leads you to a fork in the road. This fork represents your power to choose your response as to how you will proceed with your life. The fork offers an opportunity toward the path of "Overcoming" or a path toward "Becoming". Overcoming is a mindset that says I choose to not be defined by my past and I will triumph over the hardship. And to "Become" chooses a mindset that assumes more of a passive approach. This is a call out to be aware and mindful of the passive approach. When individuals decide not to stand up or speak out against the offense or the offender; they often consciously or subconsciously enter into agreement and ultimately wind up mimicking the offense or the offender in some form or fashion. Please know that agreements are powerful. Choosing to "Overcome" yields personal growth and freedom. This space of growth helps you to help others. The more you evolve; you serve as light and hope to others. Ask me – I know.

God continues to heal and use me as a vessel. And, I have become a confidant to many. It doesn't matter where I am in the world people take comfort in approaching me and sharing their life with me. From old to young, Ministers, to Executives, to Students literally every walk of life. And, I count this as an honor that individuals see God's light within me. As I have listened to their journeys, I have observed a semblance in many of them and that semblance was either they'd Become or Overcome their situations. Here's a playback of a conversation that I had with a young lady. Unbeknownst to her…. she had "Become" her stepfather.

What You Do Not Overcome – You Become

Tan hated Friday nights. This is because she knew that she would be awakened by the screams of her mother. She grew up witnessing her stepfather beat her mother. Jay (Tan's stepfather) would stumble into the house as a result of having had too much to drink and/or drug use on Friday nights. It just depended on which was his poison of choice to end the week. Jay would somehow manage to get home safely after being out late. He'd stumble through the house until he made his way to the master bedroom. He'd enter the room armed and ready to start a fight. Generally, by complaining that the house wasn't clean enough or accusing her mother of something frivolous. His accusations were always ridiculous. Her mother tried to ignore him, which made him even more upset. Then it would begin. Yelling first, then the crescendo to her mother screaming because she'd been slapped and or punched in the face. It was like that of a disturbing rhythm of her stepfathers punches and then her mothers' screams. This rhythm would be on repeat for what seemed liked hours. Then the rhythm would stop, he'd collapse on to the bed and would begin to snore and her mother would weep herself to sleep. Jay would sober up on Saturday in preparation for church on Sunday. After-all he had an image to uphold, Jay was the Pastor of their church. And, boy was he proud of this. He loved authority. Tan thought he had amnesia because he'd proclaim on "Sundays" that we should love our neighbors but, he seemed to forget that he'd beat her mother two nights before.

Fortunately, Jay never unleashed his wrath directly on to Tan but, he most certainly did indirectly. Her mother was her world. Especially since Tan's father had been absent all her life and, witnessing this monster abuse her mother literally crushed Tan at her core. It was one thing to hear her mother cry out in the night and it was another thing to see the bruising on her mothers' body the mornings after. Tan hated her stepfather and he knew it. He also didn't care. He learned to skillfully ignore her stares of disgust when their eyes would meet as they would cross each other's paths in the house. And, when her mother noticed that Tan was being defiant, she would quickly correct her. Which infuriated Tan. This is because her mother had the courage to correct her, but she didn't have the courage to correct the one that was beating her. Tan tried talking to her mother and begged her to leave her stepfather but, her mother always responded with compassion toward him. This was something Tan could never understand. What Tan didn't know was that Jay's father beat him when he was a child and, Tan's mother knew this and was secretly patient and hopeful that things would change but Jay never got help nor did he take a stand regarding the abuse. Unbeknownst to Jay, he had "BECOME" his father. Years passed before the relationship with Jay and her mother ended. Although the relationship ended, the scarring from the abuse was long lasting for Tan and her mother. Not to mention, neither of them ever got help. Her mother later remarried, and Tan went out of state to college.

Life seemed to be fine. Tan began to date and later married her college sweetheart.

Unbeknownst to her, Tan began responding with rage when things did not align the way that she expected within the marriage. This behavior was familiar to her and her husband became the victim of her rage. Their insecurities fed into each other. They were both broken and wanted love but exhibited in different ways. He was timid and allowed Tan to verbally/emotionally abuse him. Tan was a bully, insecure and used rage to get her way. What was supposed to be a marriage made in heaven, wound up being an absolute recipe for disaster. Three years after enduring the ebbs and flows of marriage she found out that she was pregnant with twins. Tan birthed two plump handsome baby boys. Her husband secretly hoped that this glorious moment in their marriage would serve also as a turning point or a fresh start because he was secretly miserable, but the pain and dysfunction continued. When the twins turned nine Tan found herself in divorce court. She was blown away that the marriage was dissolving. She asked her soon to be ex-husband why he wanted a divorce. He shared that she had been a monster and he was tired of the abuse. To say that Tan was stunned was an understatement. She could not believe that she'd behaved that way. He was having a hard time believing that she was in such disbelief. Tan proceeded to share that her behavior was as a result of what she'd seen as a child. What Tan had witnessed had **"BECOME"** a part of her. It was clear to Tan that it was too late for her marriage but, she decided in that moment that it wasn't too late for her children to get help. After-all her kids had witnessed her rage and Tan was determined to be proactive to ensure that they would not "Become" like her. She found a therapist and continues to tread the path toward healing with her boys.

Think About It: Jay had become his Father and Tan had become Jay. Neither of them appreciated enduring the mistreatment from their pasts and, neither Jay nor Tan took an active stand to OVERCOME the abuse. Moving past difficult situations is a blessing and it offers relief but, we must take an active stance to stop the cycles of generational curses. Had Tan not taken an active stand the cycle of abuse would likely have continued with her boys.

Your relationship with God and therapy are methods that will support you to triumph beyond T.R.A.S.H removal. This allows room for healing. Your relationships impact your mindsets and a solid relationship with God will equip you with a mindset to OVERCOME.

Key Takeaways:

1. Which is stronger? Your relationship with television, social media, video games, money and/or your pursuit toward success? Or your relationship with God?

2. Looking back at your previous hardships – Have you Overcome or Become them?

PRINCIPLE FIVE
YOU vs. The OTHER YOU

There are two great days in a person's life –
The day we are born and the day we discover why
~ William Barclay

Your greatest struggle will never be with people nor your circumstances. The greatest struggle that you will ever encounter is in your mind. Often insecurities are the forces that fuel the discord within. These underlying emotions overwhelmingly shape your self-image and influence your behavior. So the struggle that you thought was with your mom, dad, sibling, best friend, significant other, family member, co-worker, employee, your boss, with life – you get my drift…was really the struggle within you. Like many people, you believed that you were battling an external issue, but it was really an internal one. After-all it is often easier to cast blame on other things or people. Unfortunately, very few people are emotionally aware or mature enough to look within and search themselves, so they find it easier to deflect. The insecurities within us can be manipulative and tricky. Meaning, insecurities can disguise themselves as: the need to be accepted, constantly needing to be reassured, the need to be perfect, lack of confidence, feelings that suggest you aren't good enough or despite your accomplishments – you feel like a fraud destined to be exposed. When we aren't mindful of our insecurities, we will find ourselves easily offended, afraid to explore new opportunities, anxious and even paranoid.

Let's pause for a moment. Breathe. Is this a lot to take in? Do you see yourself? This principle is yet another example of why knowing: What Do People Get – When They Get You is so important. This principle is a call out to become mindful of the insecurities within that you may or may not be aware of. It is also intended to help you better understand that the people around you have insecurities as well. Knowing this should encourage you to choose not to take things personally and ultimately extend compassion to those around you. This decision will yield a two-fold blessing; choosing not to be offended extends grace to the other person. That same grace that you extend, will be returned to you. The way that you respond to something unfortunate like, being offended, disappointed, overlooked etc. is one of the keys to healing the struggle with You versus You. You are not responsible for what someone does or the ebbs and flows of life, but you will always be responsible to how you respond. Have you ever responded in rage? Have you ever played the "I'll get you back game"? Have you ever chosen not to speak up when something or someone was hurting you? I could go on and on with lists of possible responses. The way that you respond to any situation speaks to your level of emotional maturity, wholeness, and awareness. Choosing not to acknowledge or deal with them will impair your personal development, make it difficult to develop healthy relationships etc. All of which fuel the internal spar of You vs. You. Let's take a look at what causes insecurities.

Insecurities can manifest as a result of the kind of childhood you had, past traumas, recent

experiences of failure, rejection, loneliness, social anxiety, having a critical parent or partner can all contribute to causes of insecurities. Experiences such as these can leave you with negative thoughts about yourself which become destructive inner critics. What is even more troubling is knowing that you coexist with them daily! Meaning, you wake up with them, they mingle with you throughout each day and you go to bed with them. As you can imagine, this much up closeness with a destructive critic will continue to fuel the flame of discord within you. Let us examine how to receive freedom from this.

Within this principle we will look at two keys: Exposing the Struggle Within and Your Power to Choose. Both will shift your energy and position you to live and serve at a higher expression of yourself versus a lower expression.

The Struggle within. What is it?

The struggle within is a type of conflict that can occur internally when you are unsure of who you are or why you are here. When you are unsure of who you are that serves as a huge void. Identity is imperative because it grounds you with a security that is second to none. Just to be clear, I am not talking about your identity in the world. I am talking about your God given identity. Knowing who you are in Christ will give you confidence, strengthen your self-esteem and better helps you to understand your purpose. Ya see, when you see yourself as God sees you - insecurities that suggest: that you are not enough, that you are not qualified to do this or that, the need to be perfect or the insecurities that you may have picked up along the way are immediately cancelled out. This is because your securities should come from Him. Below is a side by side comparison of your insecurities versus security in Him:

Your Insecurities:	Security in Him:
Feeling that you are not enough	You were not created to be enough; you were created to be dependent on Him
The need to be qualified to do this or that	God does not call the qualified; He qualifies the called
The need to be perfect	Your weakness is made perfect in Him

Security in Him is lasting and offers true fulfillment. Security in Him offers a wellspring of hope, peace, assurance, joy, and satisfaction. Drawing from His Well daily will open your eyes and heart more and more to who you are in Him.

An extension to knowing who you are is being clear on *why you are here.* Just so you, it is not by chance that you are here. You have been strategically placed and positioned here on earth. Each of us has an assignment to carry out. Beyond having a job, paying bills, being a parent, spouse, simply existing etc. There is purpose to your life and with that - you have an assignment to carry out. Part of that assignment is to glorify God with your life and realizing your life is not just about you. You are also here to do what you can to help others. Before you can effectively help someone else it will call for you to remove "The Mask". Whether you realize it or not, being unclear as to why you are here and battling insecurities will cause you to knowingly or unknowingly wear a mask. This mask is a byproduct of the internal spar. It helps you to hide from your truth and disappointments. Behind the mask is the "other you" and in front of it is the "you" that the world sees. The you that the world sees is generally different from the you that lives behind the mask that you showcase day in and day out. The you that the world sees is generally polished and well put-together. The you that is behind the mask struggles to navigate through the barrage of pressures of fueling the façade and the cynicism within. This tug of war cultivates a breeding ground for negative comparisons, mistrust of ourselves and the struggle within. This will further entangle you in a world of confusion and you remain unclear as to *why you are here.* Separating from the mask will be weird at first. Which makes sense because you have been accustomed to being a double agent. Although difficult at first, it will become easier as you begin to align with *who you are, why you are here* and with the real you. Surrendering to the real you is another example of freedom. Freedom because it is a place of acceptance of your imperfections, mistakes and all your junk. The beautiful part is knowing that God can clean you up and use all of it for His Glory.

Know that you have the power to choose!
Choose to be set free from the internal struggle. Choose truth. Choose peace. Choose to be happy. Choose growth. Choose to do the work. Each of these choices will require work on your part. Here it is, healing from the internal spar will call for exposure of the deficiencies and insecurities. Just in case you are still discovering what your insecurities are (because you most certainly have them) . Review the listing below to see which ones possibly resonate with you. Healing begins with choosing to admit. Recite aloud the short list of deficiencies below. The one(s) that applies to you

will automatically resonate with you.

- I admit that there were times that I should have used my voice and spoke up for myself but, I did not
- I admit that there were times when my outburst to a given situation created discord between me and someone else
- I admit that I am or was hurting because I had an expectation for him or her to fix my life
- I admit that I expected for him/her/them to make me feel better or to make me happy
- I admit that I am/was hurting because things did not turn out the way that I expected
- I admit that I had or am having a difficult time accepting my life for what it is
- I admit that I hoped that – that person would behave or respond in a way that

better suited me but, when that did not happen, I became upset
- I admit that I denied my truth so I would be liked or accepted
- I admit that it is easier for me to deflect than face the fact that I am a part of the problem
- I admit that I expected for someone or something to be something that they are not and then resented them for being who they really are
- I admit that I wanted the illusion in my head to be true, but now I realize it is not. And it is hard for me to move on from this
- I admit I did not take the time to consider the other persons feelings or their story (hurting people – hurt). Instead, I became offended

If one of these examples resonated with you, please know that you have the power to change your narrative and choose what happens next. Will you continue with your life and the insecurity? Know that you have options. That option is a metanoia. Metanoia is defined as a radical mind shift. Which means your life can change for the greater good of your development in this moment. When this happens, you re-position yourself and become a force to be reckoned with. Take the bold step to change your narrative and your life. This will also bridge the gap between "you and the other you".

Key Takeaways:

1. **THINK ABOUT IT:** What Do People Get - When They Get… the Highest Expression of you?

2. This principal provided a short list of examples of insecurities. Begin monitoring your own deficiencies for the next 30 days and list them in your journal. Healing begins with awareness.

PRINCIPLE SIX
I AM CREATED FOR THIS!

What lies behind us, and what lies before us are tiny matters, compared to what lies within us
~ Ralph Waldo Emerson

I AM Created for this! Yes, you most certainly are. Whether your "this" is trying to figure out your path forward, career advancement, life after retirement, starting school, bankruptcy, foreclosures, facing your own health challenges or that of loved ones. Know that NOTHING is too hard for God and you have been equipped with everything you need to succeed. Within this principle is encouragement and affirmations that you can reference and that will support your daily walk. Meditating on affirmations, reading your bible daily, devotionals or other outlets that feed you spiritually will help you as you journey through this thing called life. Not to mention adding this to your daily regimen will yield tremendous benefits. One of the benefits that you will receive is a stronger relationship with Him. Let me just say, a stronger relationship with Him is the pinnacle to life. When you are in relationship with God; you receive peace, love and more of His grace. There is nothing in this life like His peace, love, and grace. Be sure to add on to this list as you journey forward.

Daily Encouragement:

- God's grace has already gone ahead of you. That means your entire life has already been mapped out. Literally every intricacy. So, the trials that may have taken your breath away and surprised you…were not surprises to Him. That should offer you great comfort because it is a clear indication that you are not alone and that He is in control.
- Take a moment to think back over your life, His grace has kept you. Imagine letting go of the regrets from yesterday. Also, imagine separating from the worry and anxiety of what could happen tomorrow.

Then, entering the space of now...you connect with the truth of just how great you are and just how good God is. Aligning with the truth of who you are and whose you are will change the trajectory of your life.
- There is so much depth to you, coupled with endless possibilities. Whether this is your first-time hearing this or if you are in need of a reminder, it is true...there is a lot to you. Harness this truth and continue pushing forward.

Daily Affirmations:

- I choose to renew my mind daily. Being transformed by the renewing of my mind is a choice that I choose to make.

    Imagine a "Renewed Mind" being like that of a Divine Exchange. It is the act of you exchanging any hurt, doubt, fear, rebellion, confusion, unforgiveness, self-centeredness, lust, bitterness, etc. for the mind of Christ. With the mind of Christ, you view your life and every challenge from His perspective. That perspective helps you to focus on the purpose of your life and not on your pain. Ultimately, positioning you to possess the ability to soar above your circumstances and problems and not get buried under them.

- I can do all things through Christ which strengthens me.
- God, thank you for helping me to care more about the relationships that you have blessed me with than being right.
- God has plans for me, plans to prosper me and to bring me an expected end and He will uplift and give me hope.

Key Takeaways:

- Add a minimum of 5 encouragements within the next 7 days.
- Ad a minimum of 5 Affirmations here within the next 7 days.

PRINCIPLE SEVEN
LIVE WELL!

The really important thing is not to live, but to live well
~ Socrates

Live Well! Have you ever stopped to think about just how important it is to "LIVE WELL"? Depending on the season that you have embarked upon in your life, the answer could be yes, no, or never thought about it. It is my prayer that this principal along with the previous six causes you to pause and think about every decision that you make and the decisions that you don't make with regards to your health and well-being. There are many components to Living Well. Within this book we have touched on mental, emotional and spiritual Well-being. This principal will inspire toward achieving optimal health and eating well.

It will also encourage you to separate from potentially tolerating a mediocre lifestyle. When you choose to live a mediocre life with regards to your health, you sell yourself short. Selling yourself short in any capacity is not ok, but, especially not ok with regards to your health. For instance, settling for lower levels of energy, poor sleep (sleeping for hours and waking up fatigued) , brain fog, ignoring unhealthy weight gain, feeling just ok within your body and chronic illnesses are examples of mediocre type lifestyles. It is unfortunate but, this reality is common to many. Just in case you did not know - it is possible to THRIVE in the area of health. What does Thriving feel and look like? Thriving is most certainly aligned with Living Well! To Thrive in health calls for a proactive approach toward proper nutrition, hydration and exercise. All of which enhance productivity, improves mobility, blood flow, mental clarity, reduces stress, disease prevention, weight management and works to improve your overall quality of life. Making the decision to thrive or continue thriving is one of the best gifts that you will ever give yourself.

Within this principle we will explore what Living Well is and we will discuss the importance of Eating Well and Thriving in your life.

Living Well is a way of life.

It is not a diet, fad or quick weight loss tactic. It is self-love and self-care. Which means loving yourself enough to commit to live a life of wellness which improves your overall well-being. After-all every day that you wake up – you are graced with another opportunity and that is to LIVE. Consider LIVING WELL in every aspect of your life!

One of the ways to achieve optimal health and thrive is to Eat Well!

Think about it: absolutely everything that you eat has the potential to heal or harm your body. Literally every time you chew or drink anything- you are making an impact to your overall health. Like many of you, I rarely stopped to think about how the foods that I was consuming impacted me earlier in my life. Not to mention, I was suffering from digestive issues for many years and ignored this. I ignored it because I was very busy with being busy with life and paid very little attention to what was happening within my body. I have since begun to pause and listen to my body and how it responds after I eat certain foods. Which has caused me to become more mindful of what I eat at each meal. And, has also caused me to realize not all foods align with my body. Thus, has opened my eyes to experiencing food in a whole new way. For example, I am totally committed to healing my body via natural remedies by starting with what I eat. I literally take the time to really consider what I am eating. I also stop to think about the amount of nutrients that are in a particular item. Then after, I eat that particular item, I take the time to think about how it made me feel. How well does the item digest, did it make me feel lethargic etc. Learning to eat well has been pivotal in my life's transformation and continues to help to heal my body. I also want to share that I had the option to begin taking prescription drugs, or supplements. But I intentionally chose to focus on the source of what will sustain and enhance the health of my body – and that base line is Food. Many of the nutrients that are derived from supplements are also in food. I want to be clear; I am not suggesting that individuals should stop taking supplements, I am however, suggesting that individuals should focus more on getting nutrients from the foods that they consume. After reading this snip it of my journey toward learning to eat well, you may be thinking that – that is a lot of work. Or does it really take all of that? Five years ago, my response would have been "no". But that is because I didn't care that I was selling myself short and settling for mediocre health. Today, my response is… yes, it is worth it to do the work. With that, I have become mindful that I need to consume foods high in fiber and exercise regularly to heal my digestive system. Which meant many of the starchy- fatty foods that were on my quick go to list had to be shifted to minimal consumption. Keep in mind, I still enjoy my favorites from time to time, but now I care more about a well-balanced diet that supports my desire to separate from mediocre health and shift toward Living and

Being Well. This work involved a radical mindset shift. This change in mindset involved learning to shop and cook healthy foods. I also have a greater appreciation for food by understanding the importance and the purpose of it. And that is to fuel my body so it can function according to purpose. The results are truly the difference. I am experiencing clearer skin, no acne, no bloating, I wake up rested, enhanced mental clarity, my energy levels are thru the roof and my body just flat out feels really good!

What's your story? Are you solid on calorie counting, above average with your nutrient intake and all-in with eating the foods that cultivate optimal health for you? If so, Congratulations and High Five. If not, keep reading. Have you potentially been ignoring how your body is feeling? Any chance, you are selling yourself short and experiencing a mediocre type lifestyle with regards to health? If this is you, know that you are not alone, and I am so grateful that you are reading this principal and I pray that it adds value to your life. Eating well is a pipeline to a better quality of life. You may have heard it before "Food is Medicine". These words are streaming through social media platforms, blogs, Health & Wellness books and have created a Movement. And that phrase is every bit of TRUE! Food possesses the power to heal or harm you. What is your breakfast, lunch and dinner regimen? What are you snacking on? Any chance you are consuming over processed foods, excessive amounts of sugar, salt, and fat? Generally, a good percentage of your diet consists of foods that you consumed when you were younger. If that is the case, are those foods serving you well? If not, through commitment and intention, you can create a new normal with regards to your diet and tread the path of Eating and Living Well. It's heart breaking to know that many individuals are unaware or choose to ignore the benefits and importance of proper nutrition. Which ultimately leads to health challenges. And health challenges in the body can create; Digestive Problems,

Inflammation, High Blood Pressure, Acne, Constipation, Gout, Migraines, Acid Reflux, Diabetes, Anorexia, Obesity (a few on this list, if unchecked will lead to chronic illnesses, disabilities or death) . It doesn't get any more real than this! All of these ailments start off with subtle symptoms that are often ignored. Ignoring what is going on within your body and developing chronic health conditions can cause you to experience a lower quality of life. Which is beyond unfortunate. Your body is a gift from God. And with that, choose to honor Him by caring for your body instead of debilitating it. Your body is a Temple and not a garbage disposal. It is vital that you become mindful of what you are consuming. Similar to the level of effort that you may be putting into researching the right places to service and care for your vehicle and/or your hair. If you aren't already, consider putting forth that same energy and intentional spirit with getting to know your body and what you are putting in it. One of the greatest offences that we commit is ignoring our health. Your time on this earth is for a set time. Choose to thrive while you are here.

Choose to Thrive!
Because the more you thrive the more your light shines. And, whether you realize it or not that light is impacting everyone around you. As you move forward on your journey toward eating and living well, be sure to schedule your annual well woman/man exams, physicals, oral exams and more. Consider, talking with your primary care physician about your health goals and how to achieve them. Remember no one will advocate for your health and well-being better than you. Ask questions. Compare your prior year screening results to the current year. Things to discuss: What changed? What improved? What Declined? Discuss natural options to correct any potential problems. Additionally, consider tracking your food consumption with a food journal daily. You can use any type of notebook, journal or there are

numerous mobile apps that are available. Choose the method that works for you. The intent here is to help you to become mindful of what you are consuming and whether or not those foods support optimal health for you. Remember, if you have been selling yourself short, that should no longer be an option!

Thank me later, I've created your Live Well starter kit! A few things that you can do every day to improve your overall health.

- Hydration – (you should consume ½ your body weight in water daily)
- Exercise Daily (stretch, walk, jog, yoga – just do something!)
- Food diary – Remember Food is Medicine!
    - Record what you are eating, and how your body responds
- Consult with your physician (Be your own Health Advocate)

Key Takeaways:

1. Think about it: What do People Get - When They are able to experience a Healthier You?

2. Record the foods that you eat for the next 30 days! List two columns to each journal entry. Column 1: "When I eat this…this happens; Column 2: "When I eat that… That happens

3. Set Your Health Goals and implement your Live Well Starter Kit (above)!

4. Email me at (tosha@toshaevans.com) and let me know what you learned, how you feel after the 30 days or which principal did you enjoy the most and why? I'd love to hear from you.

ABOUT THE AUTHOR

Knowing that I am the Apple of God's Eye brings my heart so much joy! It really is true, He who the Son sets free is free indeed. He has set me free and continues to heal my heart, mind and spirit. And, He has given me the courage to launch a Well-being Movement that has impacted individuals around the globe. I am forever grateful for that. To add to that...thru His grace I am every bit of multi-faceted. I am a Ministry Leader at my church, Author (My first book: Be Incredibly Well – Journey to a Better You... is a must read!), Empowerment Speaker, Philanthropist, Yoga Instructor and Well-being Advocate!

Like you, I have experienced some difficult seasons. Those tough seasons included mental and emotional abuse, poor self – esteem and I had no idea of what my purpose was. Discovering who I am in Christ has shifted my perspective and totally changed the game for me. As a result of that I am committed to sharing my life experiences with the hope of making a positive difference in yours. The content within this book exposes a lot of my journey and it explains why Living Well is my personal mantra. It is truly a gift from my heart to yours. It took a lot to birth What Do People Get – When They Get You…I pray that it blesses you as it has me.

When I am not educating on the importance of Well-being, you will find me enjoying time with my family or traveling. A Fun fact about me: I recently completed my first Half Marathon and am looking forward to the next one!

I am looking forward to meeting you… Be sure to visit toshaevans.com to learn more about our What Do People Get – When They Get You Empowerment Sessions. Also contact us, we would love to be added to your special events calendars to empower your teams, young adults, women's ministries, and personal development workshops with our life changing sessions.

Lots of Love,

WWW.TOSHAEVANS.COM

FINAL THOUGHTS

There are times when resources appear that present an opportunity to shift the trajectory of our lives...What Do People Get- When They Get You is one of them. Beyond being a simple and easy read... it is packed with gems of hope. Hope is something that we all need. It will help you to persevere as life continues to happen to and for you. In addition to bringing you hope, the seven introspective principles within this book; will help you to improve your attitude, to be reflective, become a better team player and strengthen your skillset. All of which, will help you to excel in many facets of your life. Taking the step toward improving any aspect of your life, will require you to do the work of looking within.

I invite you to allow What Do People Get - When They Get You to be a springboard as you journey forward into learning more about Him, who you are and who you were called to be.

REFERENCES:

- 12,000 – 50,000 Thoughts: Counting Thoughts Part 1; 2017; https://www.exploringtheproblemspace.com/new-blog/2017/1/1/counting-thoughts-part-i
- Food is Medicine: https://foodasmedicineinstitute.com/